The Prayer of Jabez™
FOR YOUNG HEARTS

BRUCE WILKINSON
and ROB SUGGS

Illustrated by SERGIO MARTINEZ

NELSON

www.tommynelson.com

A Division of Thomas Nelson, Inc.
www.ThomasNelson.com

THE PRAYER OF JABEZ™ FOR YOUNG HEARTS
Copyright © 2001 by Bruce Wilkinson

Text adaptation by Rob Suggs
Illustrations by Sergio Martinez

Published in Nashville, Tennessee, by Tommy Nelson®, a Division of Thomas Nelson, Inc.

Scripture quoted from the New King James Version (NKJV). Copyright © 1982 by
Thomas Nelson, Inc.

Library of Congress Cataloging-in-Publication Data
Wilkinson, Bruce.
    The prayer of Jabez for young hearts / Bruce Wilkinson and Rob Suggs ; illustrated
by Sergio Martinez.
      p. cm.
    Summary: Retells, in the form of a rhyme, the Old Testament story of
Jabez, who learned how powerful prayer can be.
    ISBN 0-8499-7932-3
    1. Bible. O.T. Chronicles, 1st, IV, 10–Prayers–History and criticism–Juvenile
literature. 2. Christian children–Religious life–Juvenile literature. 3. Jabez (Biblical
figure)–Juvenile literature. 4. Prayer–Christianity–Juvenile literature. [1. Bible
stories–O.T. 2. Jabez (Biblical figure) 3. Prayer. 4. Christian life.] I. Suggs, Rob. II.
Martinez, Sergio, ill. III. Title.

BS1345.6.P68 W554 2001
222'.6309505–dc21

                                                                    2001044432

Printed in the United States of America

01 02 03 04 05 WRZ 5 4 3 2

And Jabez called on the
God of Israel saying,

"Oh, that You would bless me indeed,
and enlarge my territory,
that Your hand would be with me,
and that You would keep me from evil,
that I may not cause pain!"

So God granted him what he requested.

1 CHRONICLES 4:10 (NKJV)

The family of Judah
  was blessed by the Lord.
As you'll see in the Bible,
  the names are all stored.
In the book of First Chronicles,
  there in a list,
You can read every one of them,
  if you insist.

But there's one certain name
   that stands out from the others—
A man of more honor
   than all of his brothers.
Just look under "Jabez,"
   First Chronicles Four;
You'll discover his name
   and a little bit more.

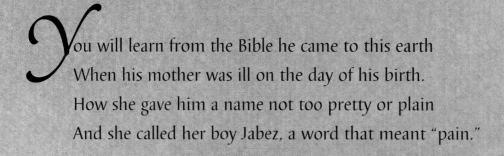

You will learn from the Bible he came to this earth
When his mother was ill on the day of his birth.
How she gave him a name not too pretty or plain
And she called her boy Jabez, a word that meant "pain."

Now it must have been challenging as the boy grew,
To reveal such a name to the people he knew,
And he would have become very grumpy and grim,
If he hadn't known God, or kept trusting in Him.

Though bullies would tease him
　　　because of his name,
He knew that God loves
　　　every child just the same.
So Jabez had hope
　　　for a better tomorrow
And offered this prayer
　　　in the midst of his sorrow:

"Please bless me, O Lord!
    Would You bless me indeed?
And enlarge all my borders.
    I'll go where You lead.
Let Your hand be upon me
    with wonderful power.
Protect me from evil,
    each day and each hour."

Now Jabez relied on this powerful prayer,
And he felt the Lord's presence each day, everywhere.
Every morning he prayed it to start out each day,
And he kept it in mind in his work and his play.

The first thing he prayed was to ask God to bless,
And he quickly forgot all his pain and distress,
For the Lord surely blessed him in wonderful ways,
Until Jabez was joyful, his heart filled with praise:

For the Lord of the heavens is also your Father!
He's never too busy—you're never a bother.
He loves when His little ones run to His throne!
We're His dearest companions, His children—His own.

And your tiniest interest,
     no matter how slim,
Can be taken to God;
     it's important to Him.
You can tell Him
     the truest desire you feel,
For He wants you to be
     very honest and real.

If you ask Him to bless you,
     He'll grant your request
With a loving reply,
     for He knows what is best.
And like Jabez, you'll feel
     so much joy and such praise,
That you'll want to serve God
     in a hundred new ways.

Now Jabez looked out on his small space and sighed,
For his land wasn't large and his borders weren't wide.
Yet he wanted to put a broad smile on God's face
And to do larger deeds which required more space.

So he asked that his borders would grow and expand
To more friends, opportunities, talents, and land.
And I hope you won't think he was selfish or greedy;
He wanted to reach out to those who were needy.

When we're serving the Father, our borders will grow,
For we're helping and healing wherever we go.
And as Jabez was thriving in wealth and in fame,
He would use it to glorify God's holy name.

His borders kept growing, then grew out some more,
And he trembled to think of the work now in store!
It was surely too much for just one little man,
And he never could do it . . . but God always can.

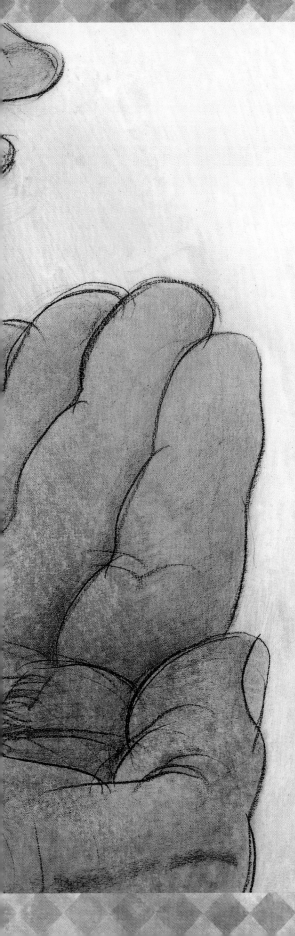

So the Father had greatly
    expanded his border,
And Jabez's heartiest thanks
    were in order.
But one certain truth he could
    now understand—
He would never succeed
    without God's mighty hand.

Yet with heavenly power,
    success was assured,
So the second request
    made him think of the third:
"Let Your hand be upon me,"
    he prayed in this part.
And he meant it sincerely;
    it came from his heart.

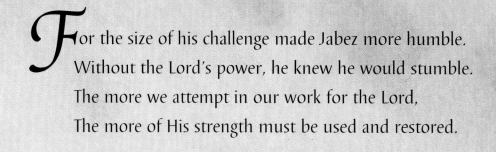

For the size of his challenge made Jabez more humble.
Without the Lord's power, he knew he would stumble.
The more we attempt in our work for the Lord,
The more of His strength must be used and restored.

So Jabez felt power in God's holy touch—
He worked for the Lord and accomplished so much.
The devil grew angry and entered this story
To fight for control of his old territory.

Now, Jabez had always been wise for a youth,
And he realized one ancient and absolute truth:
New land for the Lord means defeat for the devil!
He'll try all his tricks, for he's not on the level.

So Jabez now offered his final request
Of protection from evil and every tough test.
For the devil would tempt him to turn from God's side,
He would test his commitment and play on his pride.

The devil's a liar, deceiver, and hater.
Remember our Father is wiser and greater.
Remain close to God and rely on His power—
He'll give you the strength to prevail in that hour.

Now Jabez was faithful through each test and trial,
And he came through the storm, and it made the Lord smile.
He was proud of His child, who stood out from the others,
For Jabez won honor—much more than his brothers.

So God granted Jabez
    the things he requested,
And Jabez came through
    every time he was tested.
And that explains why
    he acquired such fame—
After thousands of years,
    we remember his name.

There he is in your Bible,
    First Chronicles Four,
Saying, "Bless me, O Lord"
    and then asking for more:
"Please increase me, O Lord,
    with wide territory,
More people and land
    I can claim for Your glory."

*I*t's a prayer to repeat
    and an action to do
And a gift from Jabez
    that comes down to you.
For that story is there
    so all people can read it;
It offers a secret,
    and you and I need it.

When you rise every morning,
    give thanks to the Lord
And throw open those vaults
    where His blessings are stored.
You can ask Him to bless you
    and give you much more.
Then just wait for surprises!
    Great things are in store!

"Please bless me, O Lord! Would You bless me indeed?
And enlarge all my borders. I'll go where You lead.
Let Your hand be upon me with wonderful power.
Protect me from evil, each day and each hour."